AF885237

LOMPOC FEDERAL PRISON INMATE PHOTOS 1980

Eric "Superman" Sturgess

Rose Of Sharon
PUBLISHING

ERIC "SUPERMAN" STURGESS

Printed Worldwide
First Printing 2025
First Edition 2025

10 9 8 7 6 5 4 3 2 1

Rose of Sharon Publishing books may be ordered through booksellers or by contacting:

Rose Of Sharon Publishing
roseofsharonpublishing.com
P.O. Box 186
Floresville, Texas 78114

ISBN: 978-1-970335-19-4 Paperback

Dedication

This book is a heartfelt dedication to the men in the California Department of Corrections and Rehabilitation, as well as those in prisons across America, who are striving to improve themselves and reunite with their loved ones. Within the confines of those prison walls, many men have been blessed with remarkable talents, and they take great pride in their creations and the stories they have to share. This humble book serves as a platform for their voices to be heard.

I have taken it upon myself to write numerous letters of support for resentencing and parole board hearings on behalf of my incarcerated friends in the California Department of Corrections and Rehabilitation. I am fully committed to assisting in their release, and these letters of support play a crucial role in that endeavor.

"The Lord has given them special skills as engravers, designers, embroiderers in blue, purple, and scarlet thread on fine linen cloth, and weavers. They excel as craftsmen and as designers," Exodus 35:35.

God bless you,
Eric "Superman" Sturgess
Psalm 91

Preface

These pictures feature an inmate named Casey, who was incarcerated at the Lompoc Federal Correctional Facility in Lompoc, California, from 1980 to 1983. He was an excellent barber while at Lompoc, according to other inmates. There are numerous group pictures located in various areas of the prison facility. One image was taken during Thanksgiving dinner and is eerily similar to the movie Goodfellas, where some Italian mafia members were in federal prison and were making their own food and having a lavish meal.

Casey and his crew seemed like a playful bunch, as evidenced by the pictures they took. Some of the photographs I can not show in this book because of their provocative nature. I don't know if Lompoc Prison had a photo club at the time where they could check out cameras and develop pictures, like other correctional facilities around this time. They took a large number of photos, and I don't know the story behind how that was possible at the time in this federal prison.

These photos are a snapshot of time that captures these men doing their best to survive behind those cold prison walls. These photos and the people in them deserve to be seen by others and their lives not forgotten in the dustbins of history. It just reminds us how fleeting our lives are. Nobody is guaranteed tomorrow, and our youth quickly fades to old age if we are blessed to live that long.

God bless you
Eric Sturgess
Romans 10:9-13

Table of Contents

Dedication....3

Preface....4

Introduction....6

Photographs....7

About the Author....43

Other Books....46

Introduction

Lompoc Federal Correctional Facility is located on the central coast of California, near farmland, coastal hills, and the Pacific Ocean. Behind its fences and barbed wire, however, the atmosphere was far removed from the calm and beauty that surrounded it. During the early 1980s, Lompoc housed a diverse population of federal inmates serving sentences for a wide range of crimes. Men involved in organized crime, drug trafficking, and major financial cases often lived alongside those whose lives had taken tragic and complicated turns.

Life inside Lompoc followed strict rules and tight schedules. Movement was controlled. Privacy was almost nonexistent. Inmates learned to navigate social hierarchies, build alliances, and maintain their own sense of respect to endure the pressures of confinement. The daily environment demanded constant awareness and mental toughness.

Despite the harsh realities, there were limited programs that offered structure and a sense of purpose. Men worked in prison industries, trained in trades such as barbering and welding, and attended education or vocational classes when allowed. These activities helped inmates hold onto elements of identity beyond their prisoner number.
Lompoc developed its own culture, shaped by the men serving time there. Friendships could be a lifeline. Humor helped ease the weight of long sentences. Every inmate searched for small moments of normalcy within a world built to confine and control. The institution stood as a reminder that while freedom was taken away, human emotion and individuality continued to exist behind concrete and steel.

Photographs

THANKSGIVING DINNER
The Poc

The Fellows
EXIT
Lompoc Fed. Prison
Macho Man

The Wrecking CREW
STORK

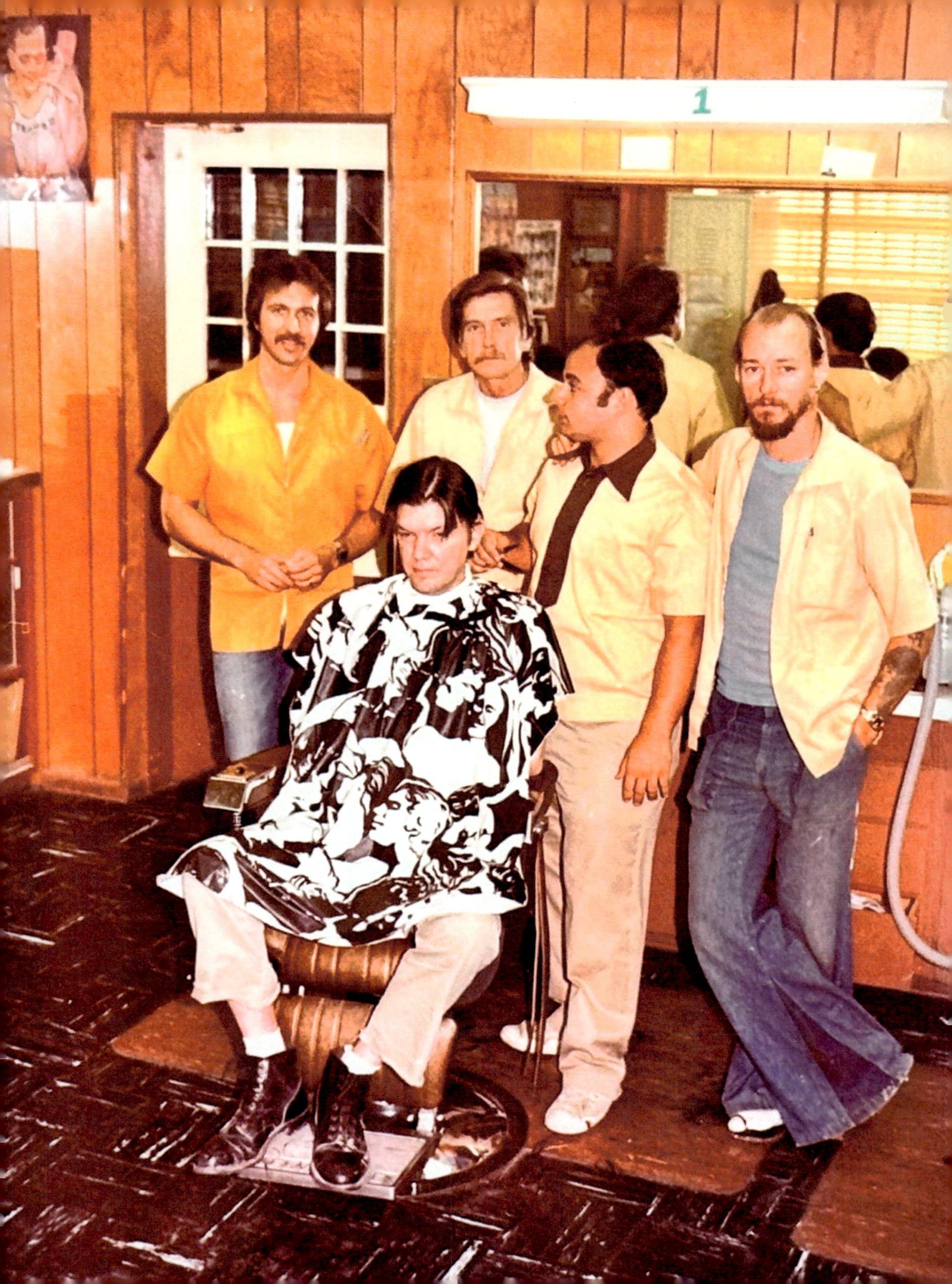
1

Buffed

10
11

DIO

EXIT

About the Author

Eric has emerged as a highly accomplished investor and Day Trader, engaging in trading activities with a substantial value of stocks annually. He enjoys the status of a dedicated husband and father, being blessed with four wonderful daughters who hold a special place in his heart. Eric's existence revolves around upholding the virtues of a devout Christian, a devoted husband, and a caring father guided by the grace of God. His journey has been transformative, considering his challenging upbringing, and he now stands as an illustrious testament to the boundless possibilities achievable through faith in God.

Eric joined a criminal street gang as a teenager, and he was eventually arrested and put in a cage at the Long Beach City Jail. He dropped out of Jordan High School in Long Beach, California, in the 10th grade. Eric eventually got on the right path by the grace of God and obtained his GED the same month that he would have graduated. He joined the United States Coast Guard at 18, and after four years of faithful service, he was honorably discharged.

The following is an excerpt from his autobiography: "California Prison Confessions." "It was a typical beautiful summer night in Long Beach, California, and the three young teens fighting in the musty garage starkly contrasted the night's serenity. A teen called Bones was thrown against a wall, and a muscular teenager nicknamed E Double (me) rushed towards him and violently punched him in his lower back. Another youth named Tim Loc held Bones against the wall during this attack. E Double's knuckles landed with a thick-sounding thud as Bones grimaced and moaned in pain from each successive blow.

There's a look of pain and fear in Bone's eyes as E Double mercilessly lands blow after blow to his kidneys. E Double has spent years hitting the heavy bag in his garage, so his punches are devastating for his age. The beating lasted a minute, and the two teens stopped attacking the unfortunate victim. Amazingly, they all shook hands and embraced each other. We were all friends, and this was our modest gang initiation into our small clique called 'Six Feet Under.'"

Our tiny neighborhood gang in North Long Beach, California, had several members of various races: White, Black, and Hispanic. The definition of a criminal street gang according to the California Penal Code is as follows: "As used in this chapter, 'criminal street gang' means any ongoing organization, association, or group of three or more persons, whether formal or informal, having as one of its primary activities the commission of one or more of the criminal acts…having a common name or common identifying sign or symbol, and whose members individually or collectively engage in or have engaged in a pattern of criminal gang activity," California Penal Code 186.22(f).

Some of our associates committed serious crimes such as burglaries, drug sales, stealing cars, carrying guns, vandalism, and assaulting people. Although we were nothing but young punks, we were a criminal street gang according to the California Penal Code.

The FBI did a study entitled "Street-Gang Mentality: A Mosaic of Remorseless Violence and Relentless Loyalty." I want to quote a relevant part concerning young males who do not have a father or other positive male role models in their lives while growing up: "All gang members lacked male role models in their households, and when they lived with their mothers, they were rarely home because of work schedules. Gang members often lived temporarily with various people. All but one gang member reported that one or more immediate family members had a criminal history or abused drugs. Gangs attracted them because of their loyalty, stability, and sense of group identity."

There is an epidemic in this country of boys masquerading as men who don't take their responsibilities as fathers seriously. Many fathers aren't involved in their children's lives; if they are, they are a horrible example of what a real man should be. One of the main factors in young men ending up in the penal system is the lack of a father or, at the very least, a positive male role model when they were growing up. Absentee fathers are causing society to pay a high price for their selfish and callous actions.

Every day, I strive to be the best dad to the four beautiful daughters God has blessed me with. I live by the motto, "Be the man you needed as a child." I will not allow the actions of physically and emotionally abusive people to define who I am or hinder my advancement in life. You can choose to be bitter or better. I strive for excellence because living well is the best response to abusive people.

Eric Sturgess

God bless you and yours.

Romans 10:9-13

For those seeking to connect with Eric or gather additional insights about his upcoming projects, please visit his official website: EricSturgess.com.

Other Books

Prison Paños: Ink On Cloth

Prison Art Paños

Prison Art Hats

California Prisons: Boxing Program History

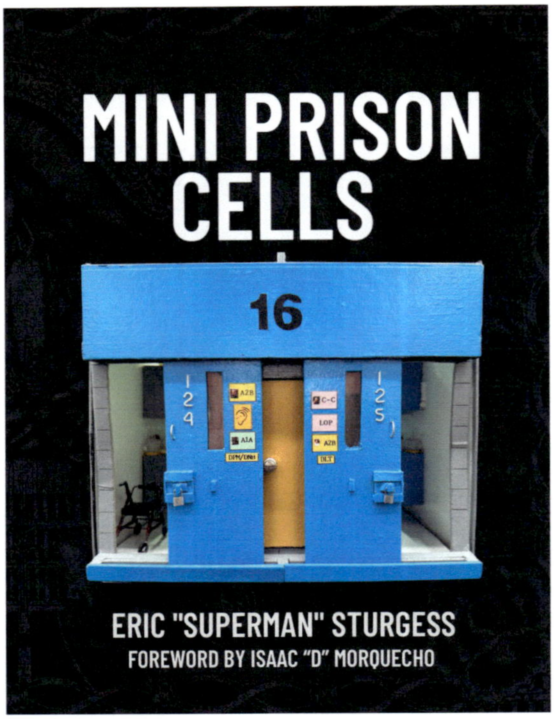

Mini Prison Cells

California Prison Polaroids

Camp Mendenhall: California Juvenile Detention Camp

Imperial Japanese Military Photos 1937

Prison Art Envelopes

Prison Slang Dictionary

U.S. Military Group Photos

Lompoc Federal Prison Inmate Photos 1980

California Prison Photos

Tehachapi Prison
Wedding: May 1976

Made in the USA
Las Vegas, NV
07 November 2026

57673715R00033